ART FOR THE HEART
MANDALAS 2

ILLUSTRATED BY
LIANNE LESLIE

For Sandy Johnson.

Thank you for introducing me to Mandalas!

Art For The Heart: Mandalas 2
Copyright © 2018 by Lianne Leslie
Cover design & Illustrations © Lianne Leslie

ISBN-13: 978-1986158633

ISBN-10: 1986158632

Thank you for purchasing my 2nd colouring book. If you want to tweet me your completed pictures or find out about my latest books I'm on twitter: @themba2day

Happy colouring!

Lianne Leslie